CALIA'S DREAM

CALIA'S DREAM

by

TARA DOMINICK

CALIA'S DREAM

CALIA'S DREAM

DISCLAIMER

Please read this disclaimer carefully before reading Calia's Dream - A Spirit guide to life written by author Tara Dominick. All information in this book is merely for educational and informational purposes. If you encounter any negative voices or harmful thoughts it is crucial to seek assistance from a qualified healthcare professional without delay. This book is not intended as a substitute for professional advice and does not create a patient/physician relationship. Should you decide to act upon any information in this book, you do so at your own risk.

The content displayed in the book is the intellectual property of Tara Dominick. You may not reuse, republish, or reprint such content without written consent.

Manuscript & Cover art
© 2024 Tara Dominick All rights reserved.
ISBN: 9798873385133

CALIA'S DREAM

CALIA'S DREAM

DEDICATION

to

Chloe & Harvey

My two shining lights.

ACKNOWLEDGMENTS

Jeremy and Pat Paul
Without the love and support of my parents my connection to Goran and my spiritual nature may never have blossomed in the way that it has. In the early days of my awakening, they held space for the unusual paradigm shifting experiences I was having; they listened, believed in the process and encouraged me to write it down. They were my true supporters always curious and interested in my spiritual work. I am eternally grateful to them both.

ALSO, MY HEARTFELT THANKS GO TO

David Shepard
For your NLP & Huna wisdom. You have played an integral part on my journey.

Jeremy Lazuras
For the expert facilitation that led to my healing & awakening.

Terry Randall
For the powerful dream translation & support at the time of writing.

My sisters Amanda, Sasha, and Sophie.
For the laughter, the love and for keeping it real.

Wendy Richardson
For your consistent support of my creative & spiritual journey, our weekly discussions have meant the world to me.

To the Sisterhood
Olof, Sara, Sinead, Louise O, Louise S, Theresa, Amanda, Claire, Ninon & Louise D for the spiritual & creative chats that have shaped & encouraged me over the years.

Bob Brimson
For your creative encouragement, editorial eye, and belief in me.

CONTENTS

FORWARD – DEAR READER	7
A LETTER FROM THE SPIRIT GORAN	18
One - YEARNING	20
Two - AWARENESS	23
Three - DELIGHT	29
Four - SAFETY	30
Five - SOUL CLEANSING	36
Six - WORK THROUGH THE HARD STUFF	40
Seven - STEER CLEAR OF DULL THINGS	44
Eight - DELIVERANCE	46
Nine - WISE OLD SOUL	47
Ten - FOCUS ATTENTION	49
Eleven - EVOLUTIONARY GODDESS	52
Twelve - NATURE'S WORK	54
Thirteen - KEEP ALIGNED	56
Fourteen - TAKE CONTROL	58
Fifteen - EXTEND KNOWLEDGE	60
Sixteen - INTEGRATION	62

CALIA'S DREAM

CONTENTS

Seventeen - WHITE LIGHT	64
Eighteen - TUNE IN	68
Nineteen - OPEN UP	70
Twenty - LIBERTY	72
Twenty-one - DELIVER FORTH	74
Twenty-two - WHOLENESS	76
Twenty-three - SETTING BOUNDARIES	78
Twenty-four - THE FLOWER WITHIN	80
Twenty-five - EXPAND	81
Twenty-six - CONNECTION	82
Twenty-seven - SILVER THREAD	84
Twenty-eight - SURPASS YOURSELF	86
Twenty-nine - RID WASTE	88
Thirty - COLLECT GEMS	90
Thirty-one - SPIRITUAL EXPRESSION	92
Thirty-two - SELF IMPOSED LIMITATIONS	94
Thirty-three - LOVE IS THE FINAL ANSWER	95

CALIA'S DREAM

CALIA'S DREAM

FORWARD

Dear Reader,

I experienced a beautiful white light in my body. The corridor was dark and yet, I was flooded with an illumination whiter and brighter than any sunlight you could ever imagine. I felt transported by the tingling presence under my skin. I felt myself becoming a part of something much bigger, a sense of oneness and peace flooded over me as I was immersed in a blissful state of unconditional love. A love without judgement, a love full of comfort and unity. It was utterly beautiful to experience, and I knew my life would never be the same again.

A year of adventures later and I found myself in an attic room speaking to a real spirit every night for a month. The notes of that conversation - which I was encouraged to take by him as we spoke, are what you will read in this book. The conversation was as real as one we might have if you were sitting in front of me now. I have not allowed anyone to change or edit Goran's words in any way and his language is like nothing else you will ever read.

Let me explain.

CALIA'S DREAM

On the surface I appear much like anyone else a busy working mum navigating the ups and downs of life. I've had an interesting career acting, teaching, and training in business. We moved to the sea when the kids were little as we wanted a simpler way of life. Being close to nature was important to us and we wanted to give that gift of connection to our children. Living by the sea really helped me to connect to my spiritual nature despite the hectic school runs and the ups and downs of married life. My 17-year marriage sadly ended in divorce in 2007, after which I brought up my two wonderful children as a single mum, living in a small cottage in Swanage with Rocky the cat.

But let's backtrack a little further for a moment - I guess as a child I was a little bit different; I didn't enjoy school, I hated being there, I felt out of sorts, and I disliked the repetitive humdrum of school routines. I was quiet and sensitive, the second eldest of four girls, I was intuitive and very self-conscious. I think I spoke to spirit back then. I have a memory of my paternal grandmother telling me I was a white witch something I didn't understand as a young girl. I also had an imaginary friend called Milly who I would talk to and play with for hours on end, but it was considered a childhood phase by my parents, and it passed.

At the age of seven I lost a grandmother figure who lived in our street. Mrs Rawlings. She invited all the children in the road to play at her house after school, it was a generational thing to have a street granny with an open house and we all loved it. We played boardgames and ate soft mints when it was raining, her two big dogs and parrot watching over us. She had a sandpit in the garden, and as I remember it now, I can still feel the sand between my toes in my white lacy school socks. She was my friend, I went there when I felt left out, so I was totally devastated when she died in a house fire. I took a year off school supposedly with some sort of lingering Glandular fever, but I now know it was grief, my world had been turned upside down and I only felt safe when at home with my mum. It was a traumatic experience and as a sensitive child I was unable to deal with it.

A bit of a rebel I roller coasted through my teens and ended up going to drama school, where we explored method acting. I loved it! We all lived in a big country house in Sheriff Hutton in Yorkshire, and we spent our time deciphering plays, creating detailed characters and going to the pub! I lived in a small farmhouse, the front door of which was in the cow shed. The benefit of this was that we were allowed an endless supply of fresh creamy milk from the vat, and the peace and quiet of the short walk across the field to school each morning had me falling in love with the countryside. This was a transformational time for me, and I really felt I had found my vocation as an actress.

CALIA'S DREAM

I married age 25 and became a young mum, we had two children and then we discovered that our second child, our son had a receptive language delay. We were very concerned because he wasn't speaking even at the age of 4 and was very much in his own world. I desperately started searching for ways to help him speak. I became a bit like Susan Sarandon in the film Lorenzo's Oil, looking for answers to help her son. I researched all sorts of treatments, and I came across something called NLP. Neuro Linguistic Programming. To explain, 'Neuro' represents the way we process information through the brain and five senses. 'Linguistic' is about the language we use and how it can affect our emotional state. 'Programming' is the habitual behaviours we have and how we can change them to benefit our experience. In short, NLP was all about how to communicate and make the most of life so I decided to learn as much as I could about it. The subject really fascinated me.

At the age of 37 I suffered a prolapsed womb and had to have a hysterectomy. I healed very well from the operation using NLP techniques to help me develop a positive mindset and I got back to normal health within six weeks. A couple of years later I was doing a further training in NLP, and they had an additional early morning Healing workshop. I was thrilled as I was very interested in all things spiritual and was actively seeking spiritual connection.

CALIA'S DREAM

Whilst the workshop leader was chanting Ancient Hawaiian Huna, I had an extra-ordinary experience. I became aware for the first time of an energetic gap in my tummy where my womb had been, an empty space - this was the first time I had felt this since the op, and it surprised me. I felt emotional and a bit shocked by this, then I felt a sudden rumbling energy coming up from the base of my spine, like a force of water, a fountain, a huge wave of tumultuous emotion. The feeling was so strong that I literally had to run from the room as I knew I was going to cry out, as I got to the door, I couldn't hold the emotion any longer and a loud primeval sound came out of my mouth, like an animal yelp and I immediately burst into tears in the hotel corridor. Luckily, I was swiftly followed out of the training room by one of the Huna facilitators who sat me down, calmed my hysteria and then expertly guided me through a healing Huna process.

The devastation I felt at the loss of my womb, now became apparent after two years of being totally at ease and fine about it. I felt in that moment the loss. Something was truly missing, the removal of my womb felt hugely significant - I felt like I had lost the seat of my creativity. The facilitator asked me some specific questions and I started receiving answers in my head, it was like hearing a voice from somewhere else. I was told that I'd had my two children in this lifetime and that I would have more children in future lives. But for now, instead, I would have a new-found resurgence of creativity - and with that knowledge came the white light.

The warmth of that wonderful white light lasted for about 25 minutes, and I basked in it, bathed in it, it was so utterly healing and loving! The bliss was immense, I felt a real sense of communion and familiarity. I am sure that this is what happens to us when we die; we cross the threshold as we leave our bodies, and our spirit moves into this loving white energy.

When I came out of the blissful state and started chatting with everyone from the workshop on the tea break, I felt like I was looking into people's souls. I felt a real love for everyone, and this loving state of connection with everyone, lasted for a few weeks with anyone I met. I felt deeply and lovingly connected to all, even strangers. It was joyous!

I know now that this undeniable white light experience was a rapid kundalini energy rising within me. I was quite simply being fast-tracked into a spiritual awakening when I least expected it. I was being shown another paradigm a field of divine consciousness a significance that I never knew existed. A parallel universe.

Almost immediately following this experience I started writing poetry, my creativity ignited, these poems came into my mind thick and fast. A title for a poem would arrive in my head out of nowhere and I would then receive an almost instant download. A complete, perfectly formed poem which I would write down immediately. My notebooks were full of them. At one point I was getting about five or six poems a day and they were arriving in my mind at the most inconvenient times; when I was swimming underwater at the pool, or out driving the kids to school or in the co-op doing my weekly shop! These poems were unlike any poetry I would normally write! They were written with unusual language, quite classical in style and I felt so privileged to be receiving them.

Then one night I had an extremely vivid dream, which I recounted to my husband who had just come back from a dream translation course. We decided to do the dream process he had learnt, to unpack the narrative and try and make some sense of it. The exercise was lucid and left us with a page full of unusual words. They were I felt, positive words and they looked like the Chapter headings of a book.

I decided to take each heading and do some automatic writing around it in the same way that I had been writing the poems. Automatic writing is when you go into a gentle trance like state and allow words to drop into your mind rather than consciously thinking about what to write.
It was at this time that I started to sense the presence of a Spirit. As I wrote, I heard a voice in my head just behind my right ear

becoming clearer and clearer. This I discovered was a mediumship process called clairaudience, and a direct channel was opening between me and spirit. I wasn't afraid as the voice was friendly it had a personality, a sense of humour too, it felt like the voice of wisdom. The tone was that of an older man, with an Eastern European accent and he told me that his name was Goran.

I am your Guardian Angel; I am the light you have seen and felt. I am shepherding you home though that will be in many years to come. I will meet you at the gate of connection.

Goran told me that my spirit's name was Calia, which I looked up in the name dictionary and to my delight it meant 'most beautiful, slender, instigator' Goran also told me that the book should be titled Calia's Dream - A Spirit guide to life.

Once the connection had been made, I wrote the book in a matter of weeks, each night once my children had been put to bed, I took to the small study at the top of the house and sat at my desk by the window. I was excited as I wrote on my computer into the early hours, starting with the chapter headings and waiting for a response from Goran. It felt quite a normal process, almost as if he was sitting in an armchair in the corner, as he shared his wonderful spiritual guidance and ideas about how to live life to the full.

CALIA'S DREAM

In our communication he said that he had been a guide of mine since I was born. That he had been alongside me at various times in my life. The white light experience I had at the healing weekend had connected me to spirit and opened a clear channel for him to be able to communicate with me.

Once the book was finished, I spent more time with Goran getting his thoughts on various subjects. I would give him a word, or a question and I would hear him respond. The writing was always deeply poetic and spiritual, not something I could or would write, but it made sense to me. Sometimes he would give me a word that was out of my vocabulary range, and I would have to look it up in the dictionary, and I was amazed that it was always correct in the context of the writing.

Calia's Dream has been locked away for twenty years. At the time of writing it, in 2004, very few people were channelling or sharing spiritual experiences in the way that they are now in 2024. Perhaps I was concerned that it might be ridiculed or considered just my imagination, so I did nothing with it. Now aged 59 I know it was a truly spiritual experience as I have had many others since, written more, taken classes in mediumship, and connected to the spirit plane in lots of other ways. Most recently I have been drawing spirit faces with my eyes shut and painting nostalgic and sometimes haunting art. My children are now adults, and my career is in transition. I have been through a tough menopause and come out the other side. I am moving into the third age, the last leg of my life so to speak.

We as individuals and as a collective have been through a lot of emotional upheaval and uncertainty through the duration of the 2020 Pandemic and the ongoing turmoil, natural disasters and conflict around the world has us searching for ways to heal the trauma in our bodies. There is a need to create balance again within our nervous systems. To find a more peaceful way to live and be. So, I decided that now would be a good time to revisit Goran's words. Many people like me are looking to find new ways to navigate the complexities of this thing called life. This book will help you return to simplicity, kindness and positive values that are so imperative to reinstate.

The wisdom Goran gave me back in 2004 is the wisdom that I still benefit from in my life right now.

It is timeless.

I hope you find Goran's poetic philosophy and spiritual perspectives enlightening. They are meant to be uplifting and helpful. He offers practical approaches to help you feel more connected at a soul level, so that you can be better directed to your full potential. The words

CALIA'S DREAM

will point you in the direction of your purpose and encourage you to create a life of meaning. They are written in chronological order, but you are also encouraged to use the book as a Wisdom oracle. Ask it questions and randomly select a page to receive fitting answers.

After a writing session I would often have to look up words the next day to fully understand them and the structure is dictated by how we interacted. There is no revision, editing or rearrangement. This is simply what passed between us.

The book starts with a letter from the Spirit Goran to you.

Much love and joy on your journey,

TARA **(Calia)**

CALIA'S DREAM

A LETTER FROM THE SPIRIT GORAN

These channelled life lessons have surfaced from the well of life, the consciousness of the divine, which is all encompassing and to which you are all either knowingly or unwittingly connected. Calia is the being's soul name, and it is through her that I write. She like many others on earth travels whilst in dream state, beyond her body to different spiritual planes.

She kindly acts as an open vessel into which I pour the 'teachings' from these dimensions, the annals of a spirit mind. What I offer is wisdom that comes from the knowledge of my many lifetimes lived, as well as my time spent in the spirit dimension.

This book has a simple title; Calia's dream. For in your dreams, you play with the hands of time, the finer distinctions of destiny, and travel to realms unknown to you, realms in which you can sense your full mastery, and enjoy your utmost potential. Your task is to connect with and enjoy this mastery in the awakened state ~ it is my sincerest wish that these words will touch your innate spiritual nature and reveal your true purpose, bringing your potential here on Earth to significant fruition.

CALIA'S DREAM

If you choose to follow the wisdom in each chapter, it will create an easier passage through life for you. So, open your mind and let my experience lie gently in your wake as you notice the impact that a deeper connection can have.

A rich tapestry of thought awaits,

Enjoy dear hearts,

GORAN

CHAPTER ONE
YEARNING

Whispers inside you, mustering now,
Listen for them, can you hear them?
Calling softly to you, tempting you, beguiling you?
Listen again, in the quiet recess of your mind,
The part of you that yearns for connection is calling.

I will describe yearning as a 'longing' for something that you intrinsically know, yet paradoxically know not. A deep-rooted pull towards the unknown. Perhaps you feel a sense of misplacement here in the present, like something is missing, something essential, something significant, that once found will make everything align within you.

How often have you longed for something that is beyond your reach? How many times have you pondered on what you have not? This causes a state of yearning within. It unsettles, it distracts, it leaves you wondering without any sense of completion. There is a continuous pull towards uncertainty, a permanent state of growing, with urgency and purpose mustering in your underbelly. Beyond you, there are many possibilities, but you fix your mind on what you think consciously will make you happy and you wonder how to achieve it. You analyse, you question, you move this way and that in your thinking. You share it, you write it down, but you are mind-numb to the answers. The answers are within, but you don't listen for them, you don't hear them. What you think will make you happy is but a misconception, a delusion, for happiness is a feeling it is not a thought. Happiness is 'becoming aware' in the moment.

Happiness is when everything comes together,
At a single point in time, meeting perfection.

Dear heart, this yearning serves a purpose, it has an intent which is to drive you to a deeper understanding of your sentient being. Lean into the yearning, listen with clarity for your true-nature's-call. Leave behind the false attributes of a status-filled life and start appreciating what lies innate within you, your truth, your spiritual quest, your given gifts.

There is a reason for your presence, your being here now in your current context, though the struggles of life may take their toll on your energy, they may leave you feeling fragile, or lost, but what better place to be. Vulnerability opens you to your real self and allows for the expulsion of the unnecessary which makes space for the expansion of spirit.

If you grasp the challenge and open to the light you hold within, relief will come. For it is in the unencumbered now, that true awareness can be uncovered and extricated, to reveal the bliss of your unlimited potential in order that it can be truly experienced in a deeply fulfilling way.

Listen, in the quiet recess of your mind,
The part of you that yearns for connection, is calling.

CALIA'S DREAM

CHAPTER TWO
AWARENESS

A thought on 'awareness' – being aware is about focus, both externally and internally, the two are quite different. The 'external' you do more readily: noticing the sunrise; the green-leafed branches swaying, caught on the breeze; the faces of people you meet; the physical dynamics of things around you. Many people live that way, quite happy for a surface existence this time around.

But now, let us talk of internal awareness. How often do you listen to your intuition? How often do you notice and take account of your gut reaction to something or someone? What is it that makes a person turn back, change course, make a sudden seemingly irrational decision that can change the course of a life?

How can you open yourself up to that unconscious awareness, where you sense a situation telepathically? We all hold this deeper awareness within, this telepathic ability. It can be tapped into in the waking state, it is simply about focus and where you choose to place it.

CALIA'S DREAM

EXERCISE

Locate that inner awareness within you now.
If you were instinctively to know, where would you place the point of intuition within your body? Where do you sense it?
Notice it there.
Feel it fully perhaps for the first time.
Give rise to it, surface it, allow its experience to become familiar to you.
Now open that intuitive awareness out, extend it from your physical being. Like a plant with tendrils opening to the sun, stretch this imaginative dynamic out, touch and connect with objects around you, feel and sense their vibration.

Take a moment.

It may feel overwhelming to use your sixth sense in this way, as you pick up the energy, the message, perhaps even the history of the items in your domain. It takes deliberation and practice to expand and journey into realms unknown but ever present, it is in the stillness of the mind, the listening ears in the very pores of your skin, that the true point of awareness is found, and brought to use.

Feel the pores in your skin wake up and revitalise, touch the air with your intuitive energetic presence. Doesn't it feel good to be so 'present' in your body?

CALIA'S DREAM

How strong and aligned do you feel?

How alive?
How centred?
How connected?
Trust this, and now found ...

Practice daily this internal connection to your intuitive self. That point within, that extends like an external radar, a light-beam that picks up signals from the energetic realm.

There is insight and knowledge to be found here. And you can see it, feel it, sense, and hear it. Can't you, now? At first it might just be slight impressions that you receive but as you practice the use of this inter-sensory tool, you will start to master the process and in so doing will find unlimited information, which you must use wisely, with the 'true heart of spiritual progress for all' as your motto.

Humanity is off balance, and it is unsettling for many people, particularly those who are open to vibration and who are committed to the learning path of their soul. This human imbalance is affecting all aspects of nature too, for your connection with the planet is deep, deeper than you will ever know. You can turn it around, but some indelible truths must be learned. Priorities must be resumed. As busy lives deteriorate and the values of relationship wane, people need to return to the art of listening, not only to others but to themselves.

Tune in and wait for your inner narrative to arrive, this is not thinking as such, these thoughts arrive without the judgement and control of the egoic mind, the deeper thought you hear is Spirit wisdom it only arrives to tell truth in its purest and simplest form and when you hear that different voice, it will be prevalent and pervasive, let it resound and resonate fully, give it time, and fully listen to the message, for it is meant for you and is a precious gift from spirit.

Once you understand how to listen without judgement you can use this communication skill to truly hear those people that you choose to spend your time with. Whether they are family, loved ones, work colleagues, or a stranger on a bench you can enjoy every aspect of their personality, their individual uniqueness. Be fully present with them. These people/spirits are brought to meet you in that day, that moment, each-and-every contact is written within the conscript of your lifeline, it is meant, if only for a brief interaction, so join them in thought and appreciate their beautiful spirit within, experience their unique expression through being open to witness it.

Talking negatively about people.

Do not de-value others or yourself with negative thought waves, these thought waves are powerful and can diminish a person's spirit even if that person is not present. The waves energetically harm their self-worth and at worst destroy their heart essence. The vibration of negativity is catching, do not succumb. Keep clear your own channels, release the darkness associated with betrayal, mistrust, anger, jealousy, guilt, sadness, and failure. Work to release these feelings. They are energetic debris, that have collated in your aura because of your lived experience. They fetter your soul and are imposters to your pure state of being.

However, it is well to remember that those lived experiences though challenging are part of the path to understanding your soul's purpose. Take the learnings then clear away the negative debris that stops the clarity of your vision appearing. Live from a place of light and use that light-heartedness to protect yourself when in the firing-line of others.

Restoration for humanity is needed, it will be found not through religion, nor politics, nor money, nor alien saviours but through a simple means of personal clarity and perspective within the masses. Encompass these elements of spirit wisdom into your own life and you cannot help but supremely affect the lives of those around you, the collective energy field.

CALIA'S DREAM

*The words in Calia's Dream are full of inner truths,
simplistic gifts that when re-opened and re-read,
will delight you and gently start to enhance the quality of your
magnificent life.*

Rise to your own significance.

CALIA'S DREAM

CHAPTER THREE
DELIGHT

Remember that feeling of childish delight when something utterly enchanted and excited you?

EXERCISE

Connect with that feeling now.
Where do you locate it in your being?
Now extend that delight outward. You may find a smile upon your face, or a tingling sensation, you may feel your inner childishness come to bear, how long since you made contact there?

Yearning for material gain and shallow success is a wrongly placed focus. When you think of 'yearning' feel the negative pull. Feel the discontent. It is pulling you off balance and before long it may topple you. Continuation in this manner must be thwarted, stopped in its tracks, for true happiness lies at the heart of you and the way to it, is through the journey of awareness and connection.

Delight in your day and create fond moments to treasure.

CHAPTER FOUR
SAFETY

It is futile to rely on others to make you feel safe. True safety comes from within. This understanding must start from the inside. Safety, feeling safe, is a number one priority. No one wants to feel in danger; instability causes fear and fear creates fearful acts.

So how do you harness stability? First it comes from knowing where you are. Honestly assessing your life's predicament.

EXERCISE

Stand firmly in the present.
A moment of atonement.
Look clearly with an honest heart.
Focus your intent and discover your current standing.
Write it down. Absorb it, accept where you are, and don't judge it.
Be kind to yourself as kindness is the appreciation of the good in you. Appreciate the goodness within yourself and notice the honesty and goodness in others.

CALIA'S DREAM

Honesty stabilizes. It stops you making rash decisions; it prevents cruel mistakes that knock the soul off its present path. Fate plays its part in your life but only in relation to your conscious choice. Your ego consciously creates a path, and the soul then takes the lessons learnt on that path. If everything happens for a reason, then reasons must provide some answers for you to ponder.

Don't expect the Universe or God to do it all for you. The Divine supports you and will endeavour to guide positive connections and opportunities your way, but you must act upon them, responsibility for the 'act' lies with you.

Safety comes from trust.

There is no need to be afraid of the afterlife as it is an energy and place already familiar to you. It is where you have come from, and it is where you will return to when you travel homeward. Returning home always feels good, doesn't it?

CALIA'S DREAM

GORAN TALK TO ME OF DEATH.

Death is profound.
An experience which resonates on many levels.
Clarity comes in the moment just before death takes your spiritual hand. It is like the opening of a flower.
At last, you can trust and allow the warmth of Heaven to open you up to a new day.
In that single moment everything makes sense.
Complete and utter peace rescues you from your mortal body, releases your physical encumbrance, and guides you homeward.

As the soul lifts and rises it takes a last look,
one last remembrance that connects at the human level.
It is as if all the love that you felt in a lifetime is concentrated and its essence is fully felt. It is a magical moment, an intense moment, a ritual passing
that many souls long to experience again and again.
For as you pass to death your journey of the lifetime chosen is complete. Rich learnings will occur when integration has taken place and full understanding absorbs and nourishes the soul's expression.
Death is about returning to the light;
it is a beautiful and rewarding experience for all.

Interpret life as a 'great trip' and one from which you will inevitably return home. So, what aspects of your trip have you enjoyed so far? What have you covered to date? How adventurous have you been in your life? Have you travelled far and wide? Have you met plenty of interesting people? Have you experienced different landscapes, swum in different waters, tasted different cuisine? Look at your life now, for what it is and what it has been. Have you experienced a varied taste of life's potential? If not, it is time to re-group your thoughts and go out and experience some adventure!

Many people think that safety comes from sticking with what you know, doing the same things in the same way, with the same people. Wrong. Safety comes from stretching your legs and walking out on your own. Internal safety comes from the knowledge of one's own external capabilities. If you could assuredly say,

I trust myself to be totally alright in any situation life presents me.
(Say it aloud).

Wouldn't that be a blessed relief? How could you not be unafraid to act upon chance, if you had that inner trust at your core? We create our own safety levels within. That is why some people feel safe and others unfortunately suffer from varying degrees of fear and anxiety, at their own hand.

EXERCISE

You know that cocooned feeling when you are wrapped up in a warm blanket? Go there now, remember a time when you were fully relaxed and safe, and notice the stillness of your mind, the comfort in your heart, your ability to trust.

Now relax your muscles and lean in a little further.

Lean into the soft holding of your inner safety.

The world's atrocities stem from humanity's inability to trust. If everyone held inner safety and absolute trust, then the world would inevitably be a kinder and safer place. Random acts of aggression stem from imbalance. Insecurity is a deeply personal response, yet humans are forever trying to get their security from others. Nurture a security within, develop your own inner security system that protects you and allows you to step into the world without fear.

Be fear-less.

Fear resists success.

It is the one true cause of failure.

If you eliminate fear then each challenging experience results in progress, any feedback from the process becomes information and resulting awareness, to be acted upon and modified until a sense of satisfaction and happiness is found. Many people take their self-worth from others, how wrong that is; listen to the words, 'self-worth' give it to yourself. It is a present, a truly personal gift. When you begin to note, how 'worth it' you are then the opinion of others pales into insignificance.

Why so keen to judge yourself?
Why so keen to judge others?

For judgment 'contains' expression, it boxes people in. All mistakes whether committed by words, actions, or negative energy transmissions from one to another are all only learnings for the soul. If you judge other people and you spot mistakes being made, then always provide the learnings to the contrary. Advise through compliment and play your part in increasing belief in others, this is how you support and contribute to humanity.

Whether you make safety your priority or not, the fact that you have read and absorbed the above musings means it will start to take effect in your life and find a place in your heart. Therefore congratulations, the process of developing your 'inner safety' and ultimate 'self-worth' has begun.

The path to safety lies within.

CHAPTER FIVE
SOUL CLEANSING

Your time on the planet earth in your present carnation has experienced much 'world trauma' be it natural or man-made. Such is the negative turn of the world that improper energy is affecting all and being absorbed into the psyche and therefore the soul. The implication of this is possibly treacherous, as souls on their return to the spirit dimension will need a thorough de-contamination of the negative impact of their time on Earth. At present this may not be a concept that you can take on easily as it is hard to connect with things of a nature foreign to you, but it is personal. It affects your soul personally and it will have an immense impact upon your larger development.

The way forward then, is to start a journey within and begin the process of 'soul cleansing' in your human dimension, now. The impact on society can be magnificent, if the world psyche begins to turn around and steer towards the positive. A process of cleansing is needed to support the simplicity of mind, body, and soul. You see even the thought of a muddled area within your outer environment will stop the clear path of positive energy coming in. This is why it is so hard for people to think positively, as clearance has not been made first, so new fresh thoughts sit on top of old stale ones. New thoughts become contaminated from beneath and slowly the fresh enthusiasm starts to seep inwards or sink like an item being drawn into sinking mud. Time to clear off the mud and clear out your environment from both within and without.

Look at what areas of thought need cleansing. What things are you holding on to in your mind that are causing a negative consequence in your body? As you know, these repeated negative thought patterns can take effect on the body. This is why you must pay close attention here. Relinquish any rumination or thought processes or memories that don't serve you. Once aware of these 'negative streams' then stand yourself in a metaphorical shower of crystalline water.

EXERCISE

Imagine it now. Feel the purity of the water wash over you in your mind's eye, washing away all the old restrictions and cleansing the palette of the mind. Feel yourself lighten and brighten.
Feel the freshness within and notice the energy return to your physical being.

Next look around you in the room, wherever your eyes rest look for anything that you can shed, sort, tidy or clean. If shedding immediately put it in the bin, or a bag to throw out. Have a bag for each room and over the next few days put in anything that needs to be discarded.

Tune your mind to notice if something needs a clean, or a wipe, or a dust and do so. Focus on anything that is dis-ordered and order it instantly it does not have to be pristine, or perfect, a little chaos and colour are always a good thing, just make it pleasing to your eye.

It will not take long; I promise working in this way will eliminate a sense of overwhelm. As you practice the art of cleansing your outer house you will find your daily life much easier to maintain.

You can then turn your attention to the cleansing of your system. Many foods are pure poison to the body. The body is the temple for the soul. What have you put into your temple today? How have you nurtured the temples in which your children's spirit resides, your loved ones? Keep to nature's food, eat fresh where you can, drink pure fluids, and notice how much better and internally cleaner you feel. Allow your body to return to its natural state. This is the biggest gift you can give yourself. Not only will you feel healthier and more alert, but you create a clearer channel for Spirit to work through you.

CALIA'S DREAM

Give it a re-set.

Give your vessel good food and drink, sunlight and water, fresh air and movement and you will sleep well at night. Keep your thoughts clean. When a negative thought arrives, cleanse in the imaginary shower of crystalline light and water. Imagine the pure water cleansing your inner and outer body as well as the energetic field around you.

The clarity of the soul depends on the way you treat it. Imagine your soul blueprint is like the skeleton of a complete leaf. You know those ones you chance upon on Autumn walks that glisten in the sunlight. See how perfectly formed they are, a replica, a trace of the original body of the leaf, yet somehow transparent and incredibly beautiful.

Watch how they dance gently in the wind; see how they float on the breeze of life. This is like the imprint of your soul. Locate that inner imprint of yourself now.
This imprint is the essence of who you are.

Respect it.

CHAPTER SIX
WORK THROUGH THE HARD STUFF

Par for the course in life is the appearance of challenges. Times when obstacles occur, often just when you thought you were getting somewhere. There are times when you question your own judgment or wonder if you may have said the wrong thing, taken the wrong stance, or simply behaved badly. Sometimes it appears that there are some people who seem sent to try us. There you are, quite happily following your path in life and someone comes along and puts a spanner in the works. They stop the natural flow of energy or so it feels. For if no obstacles appeared how smooth would your life be? And dare I say it how boring and uninteresting.

Stories abound of people who have won the lottery who have become accustomed to having everything their heart desires, but then what? There is nothing in their life to strive for, no satisfaction to be had from getting through the tough times and surviving unscathed. Usually there are learnings to pick up along the way. But learnings are useless if you don't integrate and use them in the future. We learn to benefit our Soul's evolution.

We learn about managing our own feelings when things don't go to plan. We learn how to understand the intricate patterns of human behaviour; we learn how to extend our thinking. We develop tenacity, and a structured process for dealing with challenge, we learn about increasing resilience. For some people life without challenge is no life at all. These thrill seekers: stretch their human capabilities beyond what others would presume possible. When you achieve something that no one else has achieved, it is an empowering feeling. When you find a way to do something that you thought you were unable to do, when you achieve something, against all odds, it is the ultimate reward.

So, what is it about the word empower?
And the positive feeling it gives us?

From a young age we are encouraged to do better, and work harder, be kinder, nicer, more polite, and funnier. It is as if who you 'are' is never enough. As a child, we are educated to believe that we are never where we are supposed to be in life.

To many, life is a treadmill of achievement and sadly this seed is planted early in childhood and endorsed by your educational system. When you finally get something that you've longed for you very soon start looking for something else to long for. The next best thing. This feeling of never being fully satisfied extends into all areas of

Earth life. You keep eating in the hopes that you will feel better, you spend more money in the hope that it will benefit your happiness. You focus on all the 'have nots' instead of enjoying all the haves. It's as if the human mind is programmed to not be satisfied, to not be content. Why do you think many people have extra marital affairs? How many people are not happy and looking to change their job? How many people do you meet that are fully satisfied with their lot?

The key really is to keep your life varied and full of interesting experiences. Keep your eyes open for adventure and when an opportunity presents itself (if it is not going to hurt anyone) take the time to explore it. This will satiate the yearning appetite within and encourage you to experience more. This variation in life can and will alleviate stress. People that have been close to death, though it may be a frightening experience, often find a new life purpose arises once they reflect upon it. Facing your mortality encourages a reassessment of life, a chance to re-focus the mind on what is important, prioritize values and find meaning and mission again. Many people see such an experience as a blessing which, (though hugely physically and emotionally challenging) has made a profound effect on the shaping of their 'now appreciated' life.

CALIA'S DREAM

Feeling low is a process of sitting heavily in your mind.
Get up, get out and move your body.

Release the fear that stops you from believing in yourself. Stretch your comfort zone a little each day. Notice all the good things in your life, however small and take the time to appreciate them. Set up forth-coming projects or events to look forward to. Do things that you enjoy. Take country walks, go to music clubs, read books, browse bookshops, view art, visit the sea, ramble the forests, explore new places, go to the theatre, and watch unlikely films. Take time to notice life's many creative and natural treasures. If you are not happy now, reinvent your life, rewrite your life in a way that is pleasing. How would you like it to be? Why not do this? If you don't, no one else will. Many of us wait for 'chance' to bring forth exciting opportunities, but chance does not favour the unready. Take time to care, to talk, to be interested in another's tale for it is within that interaction that loneliness dispels itself. There will always be the hard stuff to wade through and you can decide to work through it quickly or wallow in it, increasing a feeling of hardship in your life.

Within every problem is a simple nugget of truth.

CHAPTER SEVEN
STEER CLEAR OF HARD THINGS

Insipid thoughts rise from a stifled mind. There is nothing as harmful to the soul as a mind that is uninspired. A mind full of nothing. It describes no experience, it laughs at pitiful, meaningless waffle, the imagination is not stretched, not alive with creativity, not released to wander the realms of possibility. Like a trapped bird in a small cage, it sits and watches the world pass by. Unable to fly, a mind like this is living a mere portion of its potential.

Closed-in thoughts nullify existence and shorten life. This is not to say that a soul must do the most amazing things in its life, by no means take that as my intention. A simple life can be very richly lived. But it is in the treasuring of moments, the full connection of mind and body living through experience, where true satisfaction is found. How often do we half experience things? Even intense, extraordinary events are sometimes taken for granted or experienced in a state of shock instead of wonder, only realizing how great the event was in the after effect.

CALIA'S DREAM

Belittle not the striking boldness of this notion. For this chapter heading holds a key to inward success. Success is really a delicacy of the mind. Something to be personally savoured. Muse upon the face of an Olympic Athlete, who has finally reached, perhaps a childhood dream of getting a gold medal. Notice the inward focus. The absolute veracity, the relish of success.

The expectation and realization of something different provides a stimulus to the soul. A revving of adrenaline. A juicing up of emotion. It is what keeps you looking forward to tomorrow while savouring the moment of today. So how can you live like this? It is by the simple choice of steering clear of people and things that bore you.

Make a difference to your life by seeking out adventure.

Look out for new experiences and take a chance to change your outlook. Stretching one's mind can be a fun pastime. Jump the fence sometimes and take a different route. Surprise yourself with the flexibility of your thoughts. Think around subjects, explore possibilities. Delve into new areas and activate new brain paths. Deliberate on ideas, ponder, work your way along the wonderful river of life and stop off at many unexpected places.

Become a tourist guide for your soul and slumber no more.

CALIA'S DREAM

CHAPTER EIGHT
DELIVERANCE

Repeatedly ensure the decadent nature of the energy of life is present and realize the abundant nature of interaction with others, as this will bring forth deliverance.

It will bring forth deliverance of sublime life qualities, that will enlighten and illuminate your days.

*For within lies possibility beyond your measure.
It glistens like a perfect star; it hankers your attention.
It espouses your loving want and creates your outer world.
Bring forth the magic within unto deliverance.
For it is in the deliverance of your gifts that you truly pleasure life.*

CHAPTER NINE
WISE OLD SOUL

At the heart of it, we are all wise. It is just that some 'soul wisdom' is lived out in low level existence. Flexibility of thinking will enable you to accept and not tarnish the impoverished mental ability of some people in society. Theirs is a journey of progression also, it is just that their progression is lived out through physical experience and not through mind and spirit development. Big hearts are needed to provide the encouragement of these souls into the spiritual field. Because it is in the connection with the inner self that true spiritual progression in a lifetime takes place.

At reincarnation, a soul knows the life it is entering, it may have been tasked to take that life, challenged to, and it has a choice as to how to lead that life. So, as you look at all the perceived problems in your life, the financial hardships, the family upheavals, the losses, the health issues, and the frustrations, know that these are all part of the wider perspective, the never-ending progression of your existence.

CALIA'S DREAM

When are souls born? Souls have always been here and always will remain for as long as the earth exists. Many souls have chosen to reincarnate, others stay on the spirit plane. New souls are born from the infinite ~ you will know these childlike souls when you meet them. An innocence, a purity an open and experiential quality to their journey.

When you ponder the idiosyncrasy of life, when you search for ultimate answers and a meaning to it all, you may be looking for someone to provide the truth. I can't give you all the answers as only experience can tell all. There is a different dimension. It is a dimension that you blindly know and understand because it is where you have come from, and it is where you will always return, it is just consciously unavailable to you.

But listen to your wisdom now,
How softly it plays, like background music
to your ever-changing thoughts.
A constant.
Tune in to your soul wisdom, hear it.
Embrace and encompass it into your life,
And scatter it gently on the lives of others.

You are a wise old soul, let it be said.

CHAPTER TEN
FOCUS ATTENTION

As soon as you begin to focus inwardly you will notice immense changes in your life. The calm centre-of-self, rests alone, brim full of knowledge and sound advice.

Will you not listen?

Delve deeper now, go right within and feel the aching voice of your higher self, your soul. It longs to help you; it desires to guide you. It reaches out to you, it whispers to you, but you pass it by.

So gently now, ask for support from within. This is God or Good Orderly Direction as you know it! The totality of unconditional love, waiting for you, ready to be released on tap.

In my world the higher-level souls all join to create a level of Grace and by interpreting the very essence of life's lessons and extrapolating the good we reach acceptance and understanding. The love and the light, the banking of years of wisdom, all conglomerate, together as one, and hence unity and undiscovered ecstasy is felt. Uninterrupted truth, simple and pure, resonating in the highest order.

CALIA'S DREAM

That is what you call God, Allah, and Buddha - however you name it, the power is the same. How many times today have you stopped and focused within? You don't look for the peace within you. you don't seek it out. Your lives are too busy - make time. It will be time well spent.

EXERCISE

Close your eyes and shut the mind-lid, close it gently,
Allow your head to tip forward just a little
and instead of ruminating now,
be feeling led, not led by thought.
Just sense the warmth and light within.
Locate it now. It is in you.
The capacity to connect to an inner landscape of peace,
is within all people.

That is right. It is like falling off to sleep but somehow you stay alert in your stillness. How calm you are feeling now having followed the steps above? Now allow this treat daily, perhaps more than once. It is the kindest support that you can give to yourself. It is like reaping nature's bounty. It will recharge you and create balance within.

CALIA'S DREAM

Tap into the connection that you hold within your human-nature, and you will find your undisputed authentic self. Be the claimant of your true being.

In whispered light connect to the perfect sense of self.

CALIA'S DREAM

CHAPTER ELEVEN
EVOLUTIONARY GODDESS

It is customary to evoke feelings of lack in your culture. In defence of your evolution, you may become defiant here. How can we not feel that there is always something more to be had, found, and experienced?

You live in a world full of people many of which, have more than you do. Who seem to be leading the kind of life that you want to be leading. Some of you are also aware of the lack that others have in comparison to your life and yet it doesn't really touch you. It doesn't move you to take huge action or to take stock of your worth, and my dears it is imperative that you,

Appreciate the worth of your life.

I realize I may be pushing some buttons here, and that is alright because if those buttons lay un-pushed, they become immobile and the last thing you want is to become immobile. The evolutionary goddess refers to that part of you that could become; so wise, so aligned, so triumphant in all that you possess.

CALIA'S DREAM

When you think of a goddess, what image comes to mind?

Someone at the height of their physical, mental and spiritual power. Someone balanced, clever and wise, a sage of all sages a master of all?

It is the evolution of wisdom that is key here. As the world takes on its challenges the more people will become the evolutionary wise, and therein hope for the planet lies. This wisdom will not surpass you when you die; you carry wisdom with you for all time. It will not be wasted; it is always used to the very umpteenth degree within the spirit realm.

I use the word Goddess here as there is an uncomfortable sway toward the male bias in the world currently. Resulting in war and anger and indescribable feats that would not happen under a woman's touch. For the men reading this: the time is ripe to explore the yin-side of your energy. Do not be afraid to venture forth with a gentler, more nurturing approach to life. You will do society a great service by your connection with this feminine energy.

Open the door for the goddess enters.

CHAPTER TWELVE
NATURE'S NURTURE

In sourcing, your inner wisdom, you are drawn to understand the very process of nature's work to nurture all things living. Isn't that a good way to traverse the many paths of life?

Respect of humankind,
of animals,
of plants, the trees, the flowers.
Is humbling.
Respect the power of the ocean and the force of the wind.
Join the roar of thunder, bask in the warmth of the sun, notice the changing light in the sky!
Absorb what is happening around you.
Skies full of stars,
the bright white silver of the moon.
Stop and wonder.
Feel the force of nature on your cheeks.
Ground yourself. Feel the earth, the sand, the pebbles under foot, walk the different terrains of life.

CALIA'S DREAM

*Become aware of your connection with everything and everyone
that you meet, touch, and think about.
Throw a thought into the air and watch it turn to matter.
See belief as an energy that when tapped into,
can move the impossible.
Open your eyes to what is out there.
A wider perception leads to an opening of life's glory.
Live each day vibrantly and enjoy the workings of your intricate
and incredible spirit.
Love others, reach out and connect with people, deepen your
understanding of the journeys that others are making, these fellow
souls are travellers too ~ all of you having chosen
to journey in this time.
All of you are part of an infinite unity.
So, keep that knowledge present when the world tells you
otherwise.*

Acceptance of these truths will create a profound connection for you. This is your chance to impress and impact your turning society. Enjoy the expansive nature of your soul and allow your awareness the freedom to reach outwards and experience the rich colours held within your world. Natural processes are the simple answer to the question of nurture.

Nurture your nature within and without

CHAPTER THIRTEEN
KEEP ALIGNED

When alignment takes place, the reward is the absolute integration of all. The wondrous timing of the universal spirit, entering a channel of unity. Without alignment there is chaos. A disordered mind results in a disordered life. A scattered thought does not incorporate its full potential; like anything that is sprinkled randomly, it will be hit and miss whether a seed will grow, an idea takes, a collective vision achieved. When I say collective, I am speaking of all the ideas that you collate through your life, you catch them like fireflies being caught in the light and in that moment, you grasp hold of them, always building a vision for your life. Sometimes you discard them or let them free, for someone else to pick up and cherish.

Reasonable measures are needed to focus your mind on the brightest ideas. Many people miss them. They carry them but they never take them out and look at them, truthfully. How many fireflies are in your net? How many gems to be brought to fruition? So, scatter not your thoughts, instead intend to channel them. Bring together all aspects of your life. I don't deny that this is a tall order, it will take determination and harsh persistence, a driving will within, to shape your life. Let's not pretend this is an easy task. If it were, then so many others would have aligned all aspects of their very self. As for those who are so much out of alignment, they fall off the scale of decency, (they cannot hold on, so scattered is their mind), do not forget them.

Bring forth instead an ability to draw all quarters inward, to decipher the mysteries and clear up the mis-justice of the soul. It is like balancing on a tightrope, to start with you will keep falling off but when you bring your mind and body around to that thin line, the silver chord, that central thread within, again and again that is when alignment starts to form.

I won't use the word perfection here as Calia through whom I scribe had a moment of resistance when that word came through to her. Let us instead use the word honing. As you hone and practice the art of life, as you look at what is missing or needs reworking in an area, whatever context; as mastery is developed and wholeness sought, then comes with it the alignment of the mind, body, and soul.

Deep rewards for those that dare to discipline themselves.

CHAPTER FOURTEEN
TAKE CONTROL

Listen to your inner wisdom, learn from the knowledge you hold within the depths of your soul, channel the insightful thoughts that resonate at a level unseen, this, is the aim of your life. Your Soul is here to learn and evolve.

Your unique wisdom is a fortress, it stands at the heart of you, and it has many chambers to explore and passages to travel. Reach the top of the turret and you can see for miles, whilst down below lie secrets that can be discovered if only you were adventurous enough to go there. Courage is needed. For whilst you stay on the outside of the fortress, rambling around, you are merely trundling the outskirts of your life.

However, to take control of the fortress, to seize your power, to rule over your Kingdom, therein lies the answer. Once you have taken up the gauntlet and decided,

This life is mine and I am going to own it.

CALIA'S DREAM

Only then will you enjoy your full potential. It is in your actions, your unyielding purpose, your open-mindedness that allows you the privilege of your Royal certainty. For treat yourself royally and the Kingdom is yours.

CHAPTER FIFTEEN
EXTENDING KNOWLEDGE

The bald eagle sits in its nest. It harbours golden eggs beneath. It sits safe with its knowing. Then suddenly, it swoops from the nest to survey the terrain. It circles the territory and spreads its beauty wide; in its glamorous flight it wakens minds to the scope of existence. Far and wide it travels, encompassing large areas of the landscape. Expanding its territory and scanning the terrain, it takes in everything until it finally spies its sumptuous prey. It swoops without hesitation, honing-in on the fruitful catch which will feed its off-spring.

When a moment of undeniable clarity, the heart of a piece of knowledge, the touch of truth comes into your awareness, make it your duty to share it with others and not harbour it for only yourself. The spreading of knowledge is an expansion of the soul. Each person has gifts but how many dare to share their true nature in their outward performance. Let people fully come to know you. Be honest about who you are, where you have come from, what you have achieved, what interests you; then you can relax in the knowledge that you are aligned with your authentic self. How nice to be who you are without pretence.

Wouldn't the world be a simpler place to live if honesty prevailed?

CHAPTER SIXTEEN
INTEGRATION

Surpass yourself. Entrust your life's path into the hands of your dream weaver. For how can dreams come true, without the open mind in readiness. When you open to possibility the ever-present purpose of life is thrust into nature's fore. There comes a time in life when this thrust occurs, and it occurs at different times for people. As you read this you may be feeling is it my time? Of course, it is! For your timeline has brought you to this page for a reason.

To fully weave a dream - integration of the colours you hold needs to occur. By this I mean the different bright threads of your life's tapestry. The magical strands of who you are, and who you have ever been. Imagine colours in straight lines on a piece of paper. Painted with different brushes they create unusual textures. Each line representing a different aspect of your personality. To look at the whole and feel complete, one must start to weave the strands together, to integrate and blend the colours.

CALIA'S DREAM

Sometimes they will form a beautiful pattern, an exquisite image that will become your life, at other times they will merge to create a new more appropriate shade, perhaps a brighter more vivid hue.

Think of the people in your life as colours, what colour are they holding now? How does that colour make you react and respond to them?

Sometimes the colours within are dull and appear muddy, separate and segregated; this happens when life is not working. Your soul wants, and yearns for integration and completion, for it is in the fullness of life that we experience the richest harmony. We are seeking quality over quantity; it is a fine distinction.

When separation occurs, it takes a movable force to change things, sometimes it takes an outsider's eye, to see how the colours could match and team them up in a way that creates a new vision. If you are fortunate to meet such a person, take shelter in their creative insight for a while, refresh your own creative pot and absorb the fruitful energy they bring, take it in as your own.

All wisdom belongs to the collective consciousness. Be sure to lay your palette open and be ready for the colour changes in your life to occur. Invite hidden colours to become visible. Notice how you can become an expert at re-calibrating and bravely weave threads of colour into your own magical masterpiece!

CHAPTER SEVENTEEN
WHITE LIGHT

And now to the point of it all. At the very centre of your soul's expression is a glorious white light. Those that have been lucky enough to experience this light, know that life is not what it seems. They are lucky because their perspective is wider. Their belief in an afterlife is certain and their life richer for it. They have esoteric knowledge and they have experienced a beautiful glimpse of Eternity. Their innate nature has been revealed. They understand there is another way to be in this Universe - though they live within a different paradigm.

The white light when you find it is a place of complete peace. Those who have deeply touched peace, have been blessed with the true meaning of this word. It is a place of complete acceptance and love, a soul nurturing haven, a place to rest, recuperate and revive. There is a paradox though, if you are thinking how unfair I have never seen the light! The paradox is ~ that people who have reached this place will spend their life forever trying to reach it again. Some will, and you can. The possibility is open to all.

CALIA'S DREAM

The answer lies within.

To reach it – relax, go within, be patient, ask to open to the light within the deepest part of you. Release the limitations of the mind, be accepting of self, and wield an unearthly desire to stretch the parameters of your existence.

It is a process of letting go of conscious thought and trusting and embracing the spiritual nature of your being. You can ask your guides to help you get there. And they will when you are ready.

Seeing the white light is not for the faint-hearted. For it will forever change you. This is why you must be ready for an awakening to it. Spirit guides witness you without judgement, but they are all knowing. They are all accepting, as you trundle through the mistakes and hurdles of your life, your emotions taking the bashings, the hardship, the struggle. I know, it is tough my dear.

So, to be clear. Ask your guides to tune you in to this white light, close your eyes, take a deep, deep breath, and relax. Feel the expansion of your consciousness, allow it to reach out and connect with the collective waves of the divine which are all consuming, an ever-present higher consciousness.

CALIA'S DREAM

Release any limitations you have as these do not serve you and prevent you from your right to the understanding of the true nature of existence, this white light, or white love as you will feel it as such, is the biggest wonder of the world!

You may however despite repeated meditative attempts, experience the white light quite suddenly in an unexpected place, a shift like this is markedly noticeable, like a light switch being flicked on, a tuning out of the everyday and a tuning into the presence that is aligned with divinity and alive within us all.

Once held in the light, lean into it, do not be afraid, as fear will flip you out of it. Experience the vivid brightness this loving light gifts. Allow this full mind-body-spirit healing to take place. Do not be afraid. You will return into your body as you know it, you are just skipping energy fields. It is a delicate process.

You will return, but you will return forever changed.

So, keep your eyes shut and relax fully into this divine blessing and make the most of it. Let it fill your body; fully encompass the white light and feel your true spirit's presence in your neurology and how it is integrated with the wider consciousness.

CALIA'S DREAM

Feel the love and open your arms to the peace that is within.

Embrace one of life's utter mysteries and as you return, fully acknowledge, and appreciate the wonder of it all.

Now you can carry hope in your heart, you no longer need to fear death, use your time to enjoy life's lessons with an intricate understanding and knowledge of self. How much bigger the picture is when you have had a spiritual experience, even if it is only a mere glimpse? What need is there to stress over the minor details of life? Go with the flow. The white light experience may take some time for you to achieve. For some it will take a lifetime.

Patience is all,
Sit patiently with peace in your heart.
And the light will come.

CHAPTER EIGHTEEN
TUNE IN

Tumultuous pouring's of long kept thoughts litter the lily-white page. Each tumbled note carries with it such heaven, such honesty, so carefully laid at your feet. For as always it takes time to fully tune in to the soul.

In the tuning of the instrument the host finds clarity. The clear path of a life's purpose. Its direction foretold by history's story makers. Discrepancy may be felt but harness the inner voice, listen hard, release it now so that your full wisdom may be accomplished. Turning the carpet of daily life over, one notices the beautiful floor beneath. The innate carvings of the structure of a life. So intricately formed and present under your feet.

But who knows that such beauty inhabits the ground you walk on? Who dares to look beneath the surface? Who takes the risks of time and tunes in to this ultimate awareness? It is not such a well-kept secret. It is yours to share, look and you will find it, listen and you will hear the melody of your life song, trust and you will feel the angelic nature of your being, the intricate fantasy of the Heavens, fantasy because everything in your life is truly of your making.

You can create such a life for yourself!

You can decidedly choose to reap the depths of your life experience. So many are living a half-life. How many people don't notice or experience the glory of a beautiful day? You, half but notice it. Only when time permits do you soak up the essence of nature. When you absorb it intensely, time stops still, and a gasp of gentle breath captures the beauty of it all. You must become aware of your being in this awareness. You must tune in, to appreciate the totality of your human existence. Then what peace, what calm will reside within you, my dears.

Grace and unity,
You can start with this idea on earth.

CHAPTER NINETEEN
OPEN UP

It is in the discovery of your inner circle of calm that you will find the depth of your creative and spiritual expression. Think of a small problem that has been stressing you.

EXERCISE

Imagine a circular light beam passing through your body from front to back. As the imaginary beam of light penetrates from outside in, become aware of your internal presence and let a feeling of calm pervade. Feel the light beam as a circular movement, gently turning the energy within, your perception of the problem will start to change. Next allow the imagined light beam to softly enter each chakra point (crown, forehead, throat, heart, upper stomach, lower stomach & base of spine) and notice how this helps you connect to the significance of that spot. As the imagined beam touches the energy of the chakra in time you will release knowledge so deep, so profound that it will immediately throw you into an understanding of life at a higher level. Practice the beam turning clockwise and anti-clockwise.

This process will open, cleanse and release trapped energy within.

CALIA'S DREAM

Create a mind-body system that is clear of negativity. This opens a channel of connection from which you can appreciate life as a profound and significant process. Finding and expressing your Soul essence tunes your system and helps you realise your life-song.

You will become able to tune in to other Souls and join their energy if choose to. You will learn to understand the complex message in a simple expression. This enables a powerful relationship to all things mortal, and spiritual. Creating true intuitive potential. The essential notion of the spirit. The turning of time. Work with this process, develop it and harness your inner compass.

CHAPTER TWENTY
LIBERTY

Fortitude, resilience, clarity, inward respect, and clarification of Soul purpose these qualities create the perfect conditions for ultimate liberty.

The flight of the soul's path can rise to incredible heights when spiritual focus forthwith is found. Utter stillness of mind will allow the inner voice to reveal itself and when you listen, to the collective wisdom, the unfettered truth of mankind, your heart will be truly touched. Oh, my friends how ripe you will become, how open and free - what liberty!

To reach this state brings total happiness and a pure connection with universal deity. So how do you reach that privileged state of being? Let us focus on each important attribute, one at a time.

FORTITUDE ~ An aspect of perseverance but combined with the magical quality of intrinsic worth; to discover the fortitude you own, focus your mind on the very things that drive you, that inspire you, that give you your lust for life - then you will tap into your inner fortitude.

RESILIENCE ~ Is about sticking in there when times are tough. It is about getting back on the horse, it is paddling upstream, it is overcoming the second of disparity; when resilient, no storm can touch or faze you.

CLARITY ~ If you can't see what is in the water, don't step into it. Spend time cleaning your system daily. Keep your thoughts clear and sparkling, wash away the dirt of the day and feel the goodness that abounds within the purity of thought. Put time aside meditate upon the white light within, for to find and experience, the treat of soul connection, dedication is necessary!

INWARD RESPECT ~ When you respect yourself you are also respecting your soul, your entity, your universe. You are respecting the very essence of your heart; you respect your life experience. How are you experiencing life today? Are you respecting your experience or damning it? Respect is about care and reverence; it is about love and understanding. It is about living your life with integrity.

CLARIFICATION OF SOUL PURPOSE ~ The answers are within. Write daily, relax, wait for guidance to arrive on the page.

CALIA'S DREAM

CHAPTER TWENTY-ONE
DELIVER FORTH

Uncover the gifts you bring, for we all bring soul gifts to share and give to earthly existence. However, giving of self for some can be like drawing deep sap from the bark of an old tree. The outside is hard and crusted over, toughened against the winds of life. The outward appearance is one of weathered experience but underneath all of us there is the fresh and vulnerable sap of our being.

When the bark is scraped off a tree, you find beneath pure, fresh live wood. Moist and growing, drawing sustenance from the earth, the real mechanics of an ancient oak lie in its underlying substance. We must draw forth and deliver the sap from the tree?

> *How to express the substance of who you are*
> *That is the eternal question?*

What if you were to deliver forth, to fully surface and offer your gifts to the world? To truly connect with everyone, you meet. If every person you encountered, each soul ready for connection were able to give of their gift to each other, fully give, even just in small amounts, what treasured moments would occur. The lady on the till in the supermarket, the child who has lost his way, the friend whose belief is gone, the old man struggling home with his shopping.

How many people did you give to and connect with today? How many others did you disregard? Focus your awareness now. Don't be hard on yourself. You are awakening remember? I know you may feel exhausted by world events. Like you have nothing left to give. But giving is receiving, it replenishes the self.

It can be a small gift; a simple smile, a word or two, the celebration of a friend's achievement or supporting someone by being in present time with them. Forget the hurry of your life. Connect to all souls that you meet.

Unexpected gifts make for an unexpected life.
With abundance in your heart,
You can personally make the world a better place.

CHAPTER TWENTY-TWO
WHOLENESS

Interpret the process of life as an internal journey to be taken, which enables you to work towards the wholeness of your spirit. A sense of feeling healed and complete. At first you start out in life with the open heart of a child, a determination to experience life to the full, to feel life so completely and utterly. We come with that intention, to live in our true expression. To cry with rage or laugh with joy, to love with abandon and discover with an interested mind all the many wonders that life has on offer. Oh, if only one could stay so flexible, open and free.

But then the weight of life creeps in. The shadows of the mind start to edge forward, the shocking response to life's lessons, the utter contempt for human frailty start to make railroads on your troubled brow and life appears harder as time goes by.

In the beginning you come into your chosen life as an open book and on the many pages the trials, joys and tribulations are written. Life's journey and how it shapes you, how it encourages you to find your voice, your personal path is what it is all about. Then as the pages of life turn, your story takes many unexpected twists and turns. It plays with you, involving you and disappointing you, thrilling you and comforting you and when the book is nearing an end it draws many conclusions. It is as if everything pieces together and finally makes sense.

Ultimately most life journeys make a good read. For in each individual story is the unique imprint of the soul's purpose. Some people's books are shorter than others, some are lengthy novels that take time to read but the one thing all books have in common is that they all have a beginning a middle and an end. We are ultimately all complete.

So, wherever you are in your novel, whatever chapter of your life you are living right now is only a part of the whole. As you uncover the meaning of your life, whether it is a simple life or a complex life, a mundane life, or a great life full of achievement and treasures, your book will be written. You are a part of the whole and completeness is your ultimate destination.

CHAPTER TWENTY-THREE
SETTING BOUNDARIES

Boundaries are the foundation of trust. They presume a prediction within – things will be like this! Then when they are not, all hell breaks loose. We feel trampled on and violated, forgiveness sits like a hard pebble inside and wreaks havoc within our system until the violation is resolved. Boundaries keep people out and keep people in. They are our inner stalwarts – seeking to protect us, proclaiming injustice at every turn, and frightened to lay down their defence.

Boundaries keep us bound.

In the spirit world you are boundless, an unlimited freedom of experience is ever present, but mortals feel the need to close off possibility. Are boundaries necessary? What are you bound by? Of course, they are also about protection. Look at what is important to you and then notice the boundaries that you have set around that importance. Your very own personal criteria. These rules can stop productivity and adventure, they can keep you stuck.

CALIA'S DREAM

'I couldn't possibly do that!' Boundary ~ 'I am afraid of heights, flying, and dog' ~ boundaries. Religion ~ a boundary. Learning boundaries ~ boundaries in relationship, friendships, parenthood, what could you do if you really let down the self-imposed boundaries and rules you hold connected to your moral compass.

Free up!

My challenge to you would be to have as few boundaries as possible. The few that you do have make around safety.

The fewer rules you live by the more you can express your individuality and experience life.

CHAPTER TWENTY-FOUR
THE FLOWER WITHIN

In time you will learn to listen to your inner beauty.

There is a metaphorical flower that blossoms within each, and every, one of you, sitting at the centre of you is the sweet fragrance of who you are. The vulnerability of the petals, look how they blow in the wind, the complex nature, the very heart of you, the bud of your unfolding in all its glory.

Your heart is like the opening of the flower. It opens and closes depending upon who you meet. Sometimes it shuts down until the sunlight warms and coaxes out its unconditional love again. There is such innocence in a perfect flower. Such elegant truth. It is the ultimate acceptance when you touch the flower within, an elegant expression, a simple truth, and an expression of authenticity.

CHAPTER TWENTY-FIVE
EXPAND

Sometimes thoughts close in on you. They contract and bring your existence downward. When life is like this it is hard to appreciate the purpose of it all. Life is a process of understanding, as we come to know the yin and yang of it. Appreciate and accept the oppositional nature of life, the light the shade, the contraction and expansion because that is the route to achieving balance.

So, when you contract inwards you come to a point when you will need to expand again. Like breathing in and breathing out. As your lungs expand as you breathe in, think about what you take within you as you do this. What thoughts are you feeding yourself with? What is your daily fill? How much further can you expand your thoughts, what discoveries will be made when you do this?

Constrictive thoughts hamper the soul,
Reach inward and untie the thoughts that bind you.

CHAPTER TWENTY-SIX
CONNECTION

Connection is about bringing things together. It is about making sense of your life. A life without connection is very difficult. However, if there is no outward connection, very often there is inward work that is being done. A hermitic existence is essential at times. To go within and spend time alone with your reflective thoughts is only healthy when balanced with outer reach. The best approach is to have a steady balance between the two.

If you make the time to daily connect with nature, you are connecting to the rhythm of life. And is life not about finding your own rhythm? What beat works for you? What pace do you want to live your life at? How does it work when you vary the rhythm? What is your preferred rhythm? As you listen and connect to your inner drum, as you feel the heart of it and touch your soul's meaning; then will the aggravated life become calm.

Connection is about reaching out to people; it is about trusting and respecting every mortal soul that you meet unless they prove otherwise. It is about understanding and listening and hearing. It is about looking and observing and watching. It is about touching and caressing and holding. It is about being.

When connection is lost, feeling is severed.

Connection is nurturing, it feeds you, it keeps you living and alive. The focus of connection for some is limited to the practical nature of things. As you work with the principles in this book you will start to feel the wider universal connection, the expansion of meaning.

Everything is utterly linked. This is undeniable. The bigger picture is so vast, so expansive, that to contemplate it alone is a challenge. Connection is about origins. The beginning of your journey. Your origin is who you are, where do you hail from, what is this beautiful life all about!

So, contemplation is crucial for clarity, it locates and centres you on your timeline. As you turn your thoughts to the contemplation of it all, oh how your universe will open for you and a deeper perspective will be yours to own!

You will experience so much more.
A different level of connection that will light your heart forever.

CHAPTER TWENTY-SEVEN
SILVER THREAD

Resting gently within you is a silver thread. It starts above your head; it comes through your crown and out through your base. As you sit wherever you are now close your eyes and get a sense of your silver thread. For it is there present in all of us, connecting us to the collective consciousness. It is central to the path of your existence, it creates you, it contains the higher self and carries with it all the stories of lifetimes previous. The code of your soul's wider journey is embellished in this thread. Like hundreds of sparkling particles, filling and energising, this thread is the woven string of your destiny.

Connection with it comes first from the awareness of it. Start to sense it there and as that sense becomes stronger allow your imagination to visualise its presence. Feel its resonance within you and notice how your belief becomes resolute. As you focus on the humble nature of humanity, take wonder in the presence of the almighty force of existence. Recollect memories and notice how they can be brought forth from the cord to vision. Your memories from this life and from past lives lived are stored there. It only takes your focus and belief to bring them to the fore for enjoyment or understanding.

In fact, when spirit integration takes place, this is the process of attunement. Attuning to your Soul's promise. The learning thread that your soul can study and delight in. Tap into it for educational knowledge that needs an airing. Listen to the voice of the thread and take note.

This is where inner wisdom and genius is to be found.

You may notice how light you feel, as if suspended in mid-air with the silver thread of eternity running through you. If you feel movement, almost like you are swinging in the playground of humanity then all the better, you are reaching a deep understanding of the make-up of existence.

CHAPTER TWENTY-EIGHT
SURPASS YOURSELF

How expectation sits like weighted chains on our limited mindscape. If you are expecting something you deny yourself the unexpected, the unlimited possibilities that could occur. How many expectations have you placed upon yourself or others?

How many expectations have you allowed others to limit your nature by? What exactly do you think you are capable of? Once you set an expectation, you are creating a pre-supposed limitation. This is acceptable if your value of your worth is high but what for the low achievers, or the souls that are full of self-doubt, what joy for their lives?

For joy comes from experiencing new things, from increasing ability, from discovering what you have within you. What can you pull out of the bag against all odds? How are you amazing yourself in your life right now?

Delight often stems from surprise. To be delighted is an enchanted feeling. Realizing, your ability to stretch and surpass yourself is a skill that can be developed by pure determination. How to notice this moment of surpassing? Well, my dears, it is that moment just before the point of no return. Just that second before you fully commit.

Full commitment means unswerving dedication despite the obstacles and challenges that may arise. It is about deciding to see things through as they say, 'to the bitter end'.

Bitter because you may have to face fears and doubts, but when you hold and acknowledge their presence as beacons of learning that show you the way, then they become an incredible part of the journey. You realize that the nagging fears are in fact there for a purpose and the purpose is for you to look further, to delve deeper, and to discover answers that shape the rest of your life.

When you go beyond, you get to see what is 'out there', you get to discover your infinite potential and furnish your soul with unexpected accomplishment. Challenge yourself, set high goals and know when to move beyond!

Surpass yourself!

CHAPTER TWENTY-NINE
RID WASTE

Toxins within have a damaging effect on both the endurable quality of the body's mechanics and the relative areas in the mind. When the mind is full of toxic thoughts the body reaps the unwanted results. When the body is fuelled by un-fresh food it carries the burden. Any food that is deemed wastage must be cleared - and quickly. Clean your system out, imagine as you eat and drink the system is clearing itself through. Clean images, white light, clear water, washed through will enable this process to happen more quickly. Anything in your personal vicinity that needs cleaning must too be clean. As the grimy result of areas left unclean, plays havoc with your senses.

Imagine being wrapped in clean fresh white linen, eating natural food, your surroundings calm and reflective of both your inner state and the elements found in nature. Fiery colours for warmth, cool blue colours for clarity, clean white for peace and beiges and brown for grounding and connection. Add some of nature's fresh beauty like cut flowers, or smooth stones, or shells into your environment and your surroundings will naturally compliment the

CALIA'S DREAM

nature within. Once ensconced in this space, your soul can contemplate the deeper aspects of existence. Connection and clarity will be experienced and,

All is well.

CHAPTER THIRTY
COLLECT GEMS

The introspected nature of the soul is often overlooked. With attention focused on the external, the inward life of the soul can be passed by. It is often sadly only at times of trauma, grief, depression, or other inward focus moments when the soul's calling can be heard. This is because the conscious mind's defences are down creating an open path to connection.

The upward side to all this is that moving through the dark energy and into the light is a process which deepens connection to the inward gems you hold. You will find these gems inside of you at the very depths of your inner cave. Once found appreciate. Sit with and admire them, take from their healing qualities, they are gifts for you that will strengthen your journey.

Acknowledge the rarity of your presence how special and unique you are. So many people live their daily life feeling unworthy, and bad about themselves. They are not appreciating the miracle of their life, the wonder of who they are.

CALIA'S DREAM

As you become aware of your own gems, you will start to notice the gems in others. When you do, help them to become aware of them too. Bring their attention to their gifts, point them out.

Gems are found buried in the earth,
and you will find them buried deep within you.
Dig deep for the gold inside of you!

Think of gems and crystals. Why are so many people drawn to the beautiful permanence of these stones? Their colours and energetic presence resonate with the Soul. We connect to their elements. Their colour might be just what we need.

Gold brings warmth and abundance; emerald brings brightness and attention to nature at its most glorious. Ruby the depths of love, Opal brings the clarity of the mind.

Search for your gems,
You must look to find them.

CHAPTER THIRTY-ONE
SPIRITUAL EXPRESSION

Spiritual expression is the process of finding the essence of divinity within and delivering it forth into your conscious awareness. Once apparent to you, it is an all-consuming job to release what is in fact the truth of your soul's path. This can be an incredibly challenging process as you touch the realms of your spirit, the depths of your soul and uncover a real sense of knowing what needs to be done to bring that purpose into mission.

For many this can be a period of disequilibrium, unsettled feelings, ups and downs. It is like any transition period, as it moves on to the next stage there is a moment of insecurity where:

Habit wavers as courage takes hold.

Tuning in to this expression can be one of the pure joys of life, a returning to the familiar, and the unknown in a delightful conundrum of opposites. Re-tuning often happens when in life transition, a change of career or relationship direction, a re-discovering, a re-assembling of priorities and a sudden strike of clarity about who you are, why you are here and what you are going to do with this precious information.

CHAPTER THIRTY-TWO
SELF-IMPOSED LIMITATIONS

Once the rich pot of soul-expression is found and starts to be released and as the mind-body system starts to adjust and re-focus and focus on what is important to you, you will find that old habits will start to enforce their presence. Do not worry, do not fear dear friends, this is just the resilient nature of man who has a natural propensity to be resistant to change.

When you consider the nature of this self-imposed restriction then you can also realize that there is a way to free yourself from the limitations that hold you back from a completely fulfilled life. What are the thoughts that prevent you from full achievement? When they arise write them down. Bring them into awareness and then rationalize them, are they fact or fiction?

Free yourself from the ties that you bind yourself with. Only you can do this, and once responsibility aligns to its rightful owner, oh how powerful the force will be.

Discard what does not serve you.

CHAPTER THIRTY-THREE
LOVE IS THE FINAL ANSWER

And so, to the end of this missive from spirit my dears. After all the struggle, the highs and lows, the dancing the singing, the shouting and screaming, the longing and praying, the opinions, the judgements, the laughing, the crying, and the true-blue rawness of living a life, you come to an understanding, that there is only love. Yes. That's it. That is what life is simply about. Learning to love.

Love is the final answer.

For without a heart-centered premise on which to build, life can become very unfulfilled. Look upon everyone you meet, every situation, every child, every animal, insect, every powerful tree, delicate flower, and measly shrub with the eyes of love.

Work daily to open from the heart centre. Keep in touch with your inward landscape. Explore it, get to know it, learn to love it. Feel. Feel the light, the love, the joy within you, seep into warmth and contentedness.

CALIA'S DREAM

Be like a shining beacon, and let love, happiness and contentment beam out of you. Let love sit alongside the connection and belonging it brings. Touch with grace anyone who comes across your path.

LET LOVE

Let love be ever present in your being.
Let love be ever kinder in your meaning.
Let love be ever gracious in your giving.
Let love be ever thankful in your receiving.
Let love be ever playful in your smiling.
Let love be ever sacred in your seeing.
Let love be ever healing in your hearing.
Let love be ever sweeter in your sensing.
Let love be ever softer in your feeling.
Let love be ever brighter in your glowing.
Let love be ever wiser in your thinking.
Let love be ever creative in your dreaming.
Let love be ever happy in your knowing.

CALIA'S DREAM

Present in your being.
Kinder in your meaning.
Gracious in your giving.
Thankful in your receiving.
Playful in your smiling.
Sacred in your seeing.
Healing in your hearing.
Sweeter in your sensing.
Softer in your feeling.
Brighter in your glowing.
Creative in your dreaming.
Wiser in your thinking.
Happy in your knowing.

And do not forget to look into people's eyes. Acknowledge their existence, see their worth. No matter how small or big a part they play in life. For within all people, and inside every animal there is a spirit just like your own doing its very best with what it has come to be. We are all here to learn, to evolve, to become.

Enjoy dear hearts,

GORAN

CALIA'S DREAM

A BIT ABOUT CALIA

Tara Dominick is a writer, poet and artist who has fused a love of spirituality and creativity over 30 years to craft mesmerizing and soul-stirring work. Through her creative offerings she unleashes the power of her imagination, producing thought-provoking written, audio & art pieces.

Nature holds a sacred place in Tara's creative process, serving as her spiritual muse. By channelling her deep connection to the natural world, she infuses her writing and art with profound spiritual meaning and purpose. When she writes, her pen becomes a conduit for a higher realm, allowing her to create poetic narratives that transcend the conscious mind and promote peace through inspiring a sense of grace.

CALIA'S DREAM

Tara has an ability to bridge the gap between spirituality and day to day life. Her work brings unity and a feeling of belonging.

Tara lives within reach of the sea and the green forests. She has brought up two wonderful children now adults, who are both writers and a black cat called Rocky. Tara facilitates creative and soul inspired workshops and is an Inspirational Speaker. She spends much of her time painting in her garden studio, writing by the fire and narrating audio books.

The wisdom, kindness and love imparted within
Calia's Dream is much needed on the planet.
Twenty years has allowed a ripening of the celestial vine.
The time is now.
GORAN

Other offerings by **TARA DOMINICK**

CALIA'S DREAM - Oracle cards
Each card in this beautifully illustrated deck is a portal to profound insight, gentle guidance, and soul-nurturing wisdom. They serve as a bridge between the earthly realm and the divine, offering clarity, comfort, and inspiration in navigating life's twists and turns.

GRIEF SPEAKS - Oracle cards
As we search for solace and understanding, this deck seeks to enhance life after loss and find a little peace in grief.

SLEEPYLAND - Audio meditation for kids
Gentle storytelling, lovely music, and calming sounds, help to create a relaxing bedtime routine to get kids off to sleep. Age 3 – 7

PAINTINGS - TDK ART
Shop - taradominickart.etsy.com

TDK ARTISAN NOTEBOOKS
Shop - Amazon UK

MY SPIRITUAL YEAR
A journal for spiritual expression & manifestation
Shop - Amazon UK

TALKS - READINGS - WORKSHOPS
Contact Tara - taradominick.com